Wee Sing ®

Nursery Rhymes & Lullabies

by
Pamela Conn Beall
and
Susan Hagen Nipp

Illustrated
by
Nancy Spence Klein

PRICE STERN SLOAN
Los Angeles

Printed and assembled in Mexico.

DEDICATION

To Lindsay, Kyle and Nancy

(and to the Wee Singers: Hilary Beall, Andrew Gross,
Sam Klein, Erin Klein, Katie Klein and Devin Nipp,
to Tim Rarick for script development,
and to the narrator, Dallas McKennon)

Bye, Bye Baby © 1985 by Pamela Conn Beall and Susan Hagen Nipp
Hush My Child © 1985 by Susan Hagen Nipp

Copyright © 1985 by Pamela Conn Beall and Susan Hagen Nipp
Published by Price Stern Sloan, Inc.
11150 Olympic Boulevard, Suite 650
Los Angeles, California 90064

ISBN:0-8431-1438-X
PSS! ®and Wee Sing ® are registered trademarks of Price Stern Sloan, Inc.

25 24 23 22 21

PREFACE

One of the greatest gifts we can give to a child is the gift of music. As a tiny baby, he is soothed and comforted by the lullaby, and as he grows, he is charmed by the rhythm, rhyme and melody of the nursery rhyme song.

As our research began in both of these areas, a delightful world was opened to us. Lullabies have probably been sung since the beginning of time, yet collections of them are not easily found. We have included many lullabies that have survived for generations, and we wish to pass them on to future generations.

As early as the 1500s, children's rhymes were documented. Through the centuries, many were set to music and eventually put into print. As most of our early American ancestors were from Europe, so too the rhymes and music have their roots.

These historic rhymes and nursery songs seemed to have been used not only as enjoyment for children, but to express in a creative way, feelings about the environment, politics, life styles, famous people, sorrows, joys and everyday occurrences of the time. Mostly, the original meanings of the rhymes are forgotten, but the enjoyment of the enchanting words with rhythm and melody remains.

Today's children are often exposed to the wonderful heritage of nursery rhymes, but the melodies are rarely heard. Thus, we have researched in depth to find the earliest and most often notated music to these rhymes in order to pass on the tradition. The definitive information was recorded by the title of the song — the left side denoting information about the lyrics and the right referring to the melody. Many of the tunes were originally notated in higher keys and with more difficult chordal sequences. We have sometimes lowered and simplified the arrangements so they can be more easily sung.

This book has truly been a joy to research and create. We share it with you and wish you the same enchantment.

Pam Beall
Susan Nipp

TABLE OF CONTENTS

Nursery Rhymes

Lullabies

Nursery Rhymes

1744

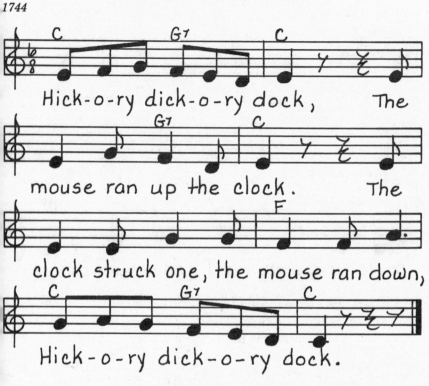

Hick-o-ry dick-o-ry dock,   The

mouse ran up the clock.   The

clock struck one, the mouse ran down,

Hick-o-ry dick-o-ry dock.

JACK AND JILL

J. W. Elliott

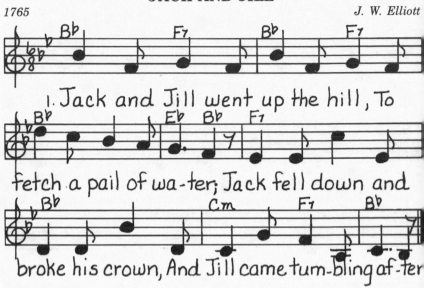

1. Jack and Jill went up the hill, To fetch a pail of wa-ter; Jack fell down and broke his crown, And Jill came tum-bling af-ter

2. Up Jack got and home did trot
   As fast as he could caper,
   Went to bed to mend his head
   With vinegar and brown paper.
3. Jill came in and she did grin
   To see his paper plaster,
   Mother, vexed, did scold her next,
   For causing Jack's disaster.

THIRTY DAYS

Thirty days hath September;
April, June and November;
All the rest have thirty-one,
Excepting February alone,
And that has twenty-eight days clear
And twenty-nine in each leap year.

THE NORTH WIND DOTH BLOW

1805

The north wind doth blow,—we soon shall have snow, And

what will poor rob-in do then? Poor thing! He'll

sit in the barn—to keep him-self warm, And

hide his head un-der his wing. Poor thing!

ONE MISTY, MOISTY MORNING

One misty, moisty morning,
 When cloudy was the weather,
I met a little old man
 Clothed all in leather.

He began to compliment,
 And I began to grin,
How do you do, and how do you do,
 And how do you do again?

1843

1. I— love lit-tle pus-sy, her coat is so warm, And—
if I don't hurt her, she'll do me no harm. I'll—
sit by the fire—and give her some food, And—
Pus-sy will love me be-cause I am good.

2. I'll pat pretty pussy and then she will purr,
   And thus show her thanks for my kindness to her.
   So I'll not pull her tail nor drive her away,
   But pussy and I very gently will play.

1. La-zy Ma-ry, will you get up, Will you get up, will you get up? La-zy Ma-ry, will you get up, Will you get up to-day?——

2. No, no, Mother, I won't get up,
    I won't get up,
    I won't get up,
   No, no, Mother, I won't get up,
    I won't get up today.

THERE WAS A LITTLE GIRL

There was a little girl, and she had a little curl
    Right in the middle of her forehead,
When she was good, she was very, very good,
    And when she was bad, she was horrid.

MARY HAD A LITTLE LAMB

Sarah J. Hale   *1830*

1. Ma-ry had a lit-tle lamb, lit-tle lamb, lit-tle lamb, Ma-ry had a lit-tle lamb, Its fleece was white as snow.

2. And everywhere that Mary went,
   Mary went, Mary went,
   Everywhere that Mary went
   The lamb was sure to go.

3. It followed her to school one day...
   Which was against the rule.

4. It made the children laugh and play...
   To see a lamb at school.

5. And so the teacher turned it out...
   But still it lingered near.

6. And waited patiently about...
   Till Mary did appear.

7. "Why does the lamb love Mary so?"...
   The eager children cry.

8. "Why, Mary loves the lamb, you know."...
   The teacher did reply.

GEORGIE PORGIE

1844   *J. W. Elliott*

Geor-gie Por-gie, pud-ding and pie,

Kissed the girls and made them cry.

When the boys came out to play,

Geor-gie Por-gie ran a-way.

GOING TO ST. IVES

As I was going to St. Ives,
    I met a man with seven wives;
Each wife had seven sacks,
    Each sack had seven cats,
Each cat had seven kits,
    Kits, cats, sacks and wives,
How many were going to St. Ives?

(one)

13

DIDDLE, DIDDLE, DUMPLING

Diddle, diddle, dumpling, my son John
Went to bed with his stockings on;
One shoe off and one shoe on,
Diddle, diddle, dumpling, my son John.

LITTLE BOY BLUE

1760

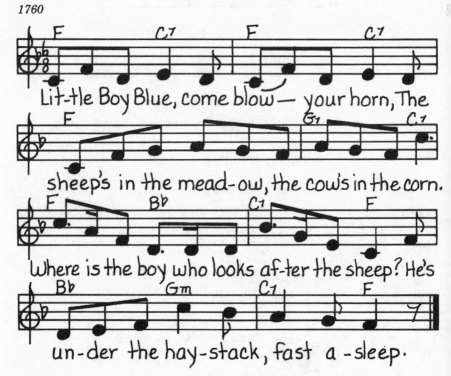

Lit-tle Boy Blue, come blow— your horn, The sheep's in the mead-ow, the cow's in the corn. Where is the boy who looks af-ter the sheep? He's un-der the hay-stack, fast a-sleep.

TO MARKET, TO MARKET

To mar-ket, to mar-ket, to buy a fat pig;

Home a-gain, home a-gain, jig-get-y jig. To

mar-ket, to mar-ket, to buy a fat hog;

Home a-gain, home a-gain, jig-get-y jog.

SIX LITTLE DUCKS

American

1. Six lit-tle ducks that I once knew,

Fat ones, skin-ny ones, fair ones too, But the

one lit-tle duck with the feath-er on his back,

He led the oth-ers with a quack, quack, quack!

Quack, quack, quack, quack, quack, quack!

He led the oth-ers with a quack, quack, quack!

2. Down to the river they would go,
   Wibble wobble, wibble wobble, to and fro,
   But the one little duck with the feather on his back,
   He led the others with a quack, quack, quack!
   Quack, quack, quack, quack, quack, quack!
   He led the others with a quack, quack, quack!

3. Home from the river they would come,
   Wibble wobble, wibble wobble, ho-hum-hum!
   But the one little duck with the feather on his back,
   He led the others with a quack, quack, quack!...

POLLY, PUT THE KETTLE ON

1794

Pol-ly put the Ket-tle on, Pol-ly put the
Ket-tle on, Pol-ly put the Ket-tle on, We'll
all have tea. Su-key take it off a-gain,
Su-key take it off a-gain, Su-key take it
off a-gain, They've all gone a-way.

OVER IN THE MEADOW

Olive A. Wadsworth   1800s   *English*

1. O-ver in the mead-ow, in the sand in the sun, Lived an old moth-er toad-ie and her lit-tle toad-ie one. "Wink!" said the moth-er; I wink!" said the one, So they winked and they blinked in the sand in the sun.

2. Over in the meadow, where the stream runs blue,
   Lived an old mother fish and her little fishes two.
   "Swim!" said the mother; "We swim!" said the two,
   So they swam and they leaped where the stream runs blue.

3. Over in the meadow, in a hole in a tree,
   Lived an old mother bluebird and her little birdies three.
   "Sing!" said the mother; "We sing!" said the three,
   So they sang and were glad in a hole in the tree.

4. Over in the meadow, in the reeds on the shore,
   Lived an old mother muskrat and her little ratties four,
   "Dive!" said the mother; "We dive!" said the four,
   So they dived and they burrowed in the reeds on the shore.

5. Over in the meadow, in a snug beehive,
   Lived a mother honey bee and her little bees five.
   "Buzz!" said the mother; "We buzz!" said the five,
   So they buzzed and they hummed in the snug beehive.

6. Over in the meadow, in a nest built of sticks,
   Lived a black mother crow and her little crows six.
   "Caw!" said the mother; "We caw!" said the six,
   So they cawed and they called in their nest built of sticks.

7. Over in the meadow, where the grass is so even,
   Lived a gay mother cricket and her little crickets seven.
   "Chirp!" said the mother, "We chirp!" said the seven,
   So they chirped cheery notes in the grass soft and even.

8. Over in the meadow, by the old mossy gate,
   Lived a brown mother lizard and her little lizards eight.
   "Bask!" said the mother, "We bask!" said the eight,
   So they basked in the sun on the old mossy gate.

9. Over in the meadow, where the quiet pools shine,
   Lived a green mother frog and her little froggies nine.
   "Croak!" said the mother; "We croak!" said the nine,
   So they croaked and they splashed where the quiet pools shine.

10. Over in the meadow, in a sly little den,
    Lived a gray mother spider, and her little spiders ten.
    "Spin!" said the mother; "We spin!" said the ten,
    So they spun lacy webs in their sly little den.

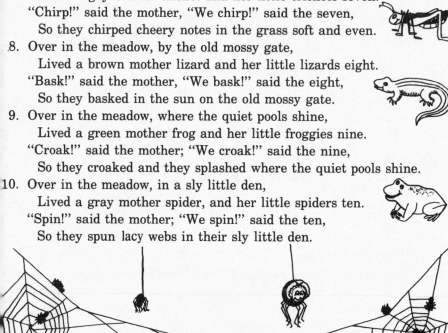

THIS OLD MAN

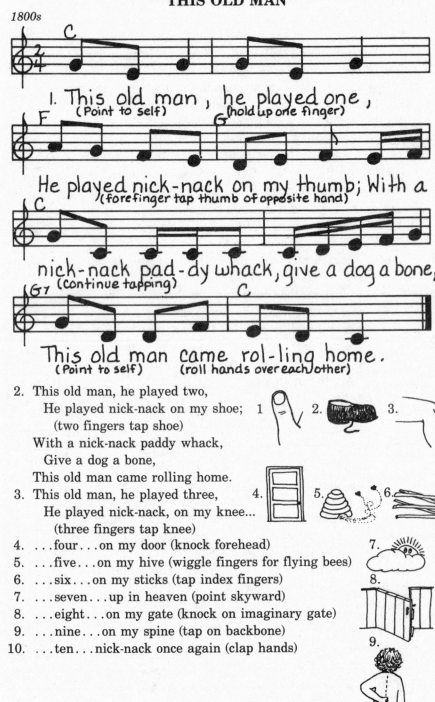

2. This old man, he played two,
   He played nick-nack on my shoe; 1
   (two fingers tap shoe)
   With a nick-nack paddy whack,
   Give a dog a bone,
   This old man came rolling home.

3. This old man, he played three,
   He played nick-nack, on my knee...
   (three fingers tap knee)

4. ...four...on my door (knock forehead)

5. ...five...on my hive (wiggle fingers for flying bees)

6. ...six...on my sticks (tap index fingers)

7. ...seven...up in heaven (point skyward)

8. ...eight...on my gate (knock on imaginary gate)

9. ...nine...on my spine (tap on backbone)

10. ...ten...nick-nack once again (clap hands)

THERE WAS A CROOKED MAN

1842   *J. W. Elliott*

There was a crook-ed man, and he walked a crook-ed mile, He found a crook-ed six-pence up-on a crook-ed stile; He bought a crook-ed cat, which caught a crook-ed mouse, And they all lived to-geth-er in a crook-ed lit-tle house.

DOCTOR FOSTER

Doctor Foster went to Gloucester
  In a shower of rain;
He stepped in a puddle right up to his middle
  And never went there again.

SEE-SAW, SACRA-DOWN

See-saw, sac-ra-down, Which is the way to Lon-don town? One foot up and one foot down, This is the way to Lon-don town.

BAA, BAA, BLACK SHEEP

1744

French

Baa, baa, black sheep, have you an-y wool? yes, sir, yes, sir, three bags full; One for my mas-ter, one for my dame, And one for the lit-tle boy who lives down the lane.

LITTLE BO PEEP

1810

J. W. Elliott

1. Lit-tle Bo-Peep has lost her sheep, And can't tell where — to find them; Leave them a-lone, and they'll come home, Wag-ging their tails — be-hind them.

2. Little Bo-Peep fell fast asleep,
    And dreamt she heard them bleating;
   When she awoke, she found it a joke,
    For they were still a fleeting.
3. Then up she took her little crook,
    Determined for to find them;
   What was her joy to see them there,
    Wagging their tails behind them.

FROM WIBBLETON TO WOBBLETON

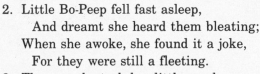

From Wibbleton to Wobbleton is fifteen miles,
From Wobbleton to Wibbleton is fifteen miles,
From Wibbleton to Wobbleton,
 From Wobbleton to Wibbleton,
From Wibbleton to Wobbleton is fifteen miles.

RIDE A COCK-HORSE

1784

J. W. Elliott

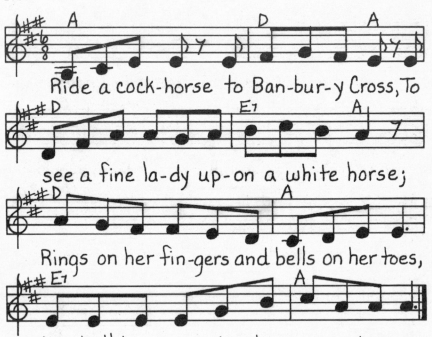

Ride a cock-horse to Ban-bur-y Cross, To

see a fine la-dy up-on a white horse;

Rings on her fin-gers and bells on her toes,

She shall have mu-sic where-ev-er she goes.

PUSSY-CAT, PUSSY-CAT

1805

J. W. Elliott

Pus-sy-cat, pus-sy-cat, where have you been?

I've been to Lon-don to vi-sit the Queen.

Pus-sy-cat, pus-sy-cat, what did you there? I

fright-ened a lit-tle mouse un-der her chair.

MARY, MARY

1744

J. W. Elliott

Ma-ry, Ma-ry, quite con-trar-y, How does your gar-den

grow? With sil-ver bells and cock-le shells and

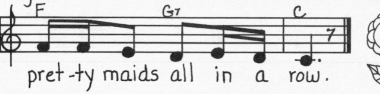

pret-ty maids all in a row.

RUB-A-DUB-DUB

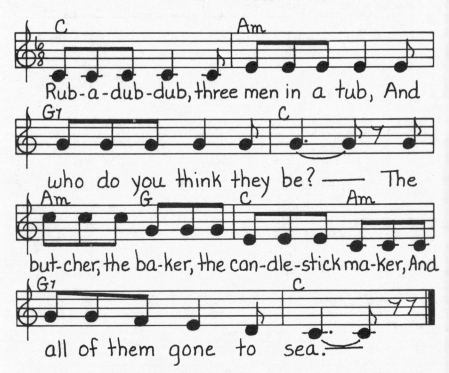

Rub-a-dub-dub, three men in a tub, And who do you think they be? —— The but-cher, the ba-ker, the can-dle-stick ma-ker, And all of them gone to sea.

THIS LITTLE PIG WENT TO MARKET

(wiggle child's big toe) This lit-tle pig went to mar-ket,

(wiggle second toe) This lit-tle pig stayed at home,

(wiggle third toe) This lit-tle pig had — roast beef,

(wiggle fourth toe) This lit-tle pig had — none, And

this lit-tle pig cried, "Wee-wee-wee-wee-wee," (wiggle little toe)

All the way home.

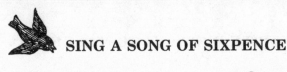

SING A SONG OF SIXPENCE

1500s

J. W. Elliott

1. Sing a song of six-pence, a pock-et full of rye,

Four and twen-ty black-birds baked in a pie;

When the pie was o-pened, the birds be-gan to sing,

Was-n't that a dain-ty dish to set be-fore the King?

2. The King was in his counting house,
   Counting out his money,
   The Queen was in the parlour,
   Eating bread and honey,
   The maid was in the garden,
   Hanging out the clothes,
   There came a little blackbird
   And pecked off her nose.

End of story:

They sent for the king's doctor
   Who sewed it on again,
And he sewed it on so neatly,
   The seam was never seen.

I HAD A LITTLE NUT TREE

1797

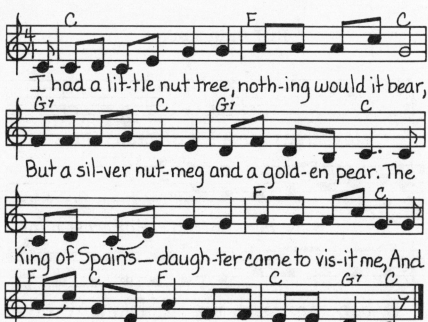

I had a lit-tle nut tree, noth-ing would it bear,

But a sil-ver nut-meg and a gold-en pear. The

King of Spain's—daugh-ter came to vis-it me, And

all—for the sake of my lit-tle nut tree.

JACK, BE NIMBLE

Jack, be nimble,
Jack, be quick;
Jack, jump over
the candlestick.

HOT CROSS BUNS

1797

Hot cross buns! Hot cross buns!

One a pen-ny, two a pen-ny, Hot cross buns!

If you have no daugh-ters, If you have no daugh-ters,

If you have no daugh-ters, Give them to your sons,

But if you have none of these — lit-tle elves,

Then— you must eat— them— all your-selves.

PEASE PORRIDGE HOT

1797

Pease por-ridge hot, Pease por-ridge cold,

Pease por-ridge in the pot, Nine days old.

Some like it hot, Some like it cold,

Some like it in the pot, Nine days old.

BETTY BOTTER

Betty Botter bought some butter,
  "But," she said, "the butter's bitter;
If I put it in my batter,
  It will make my batter bitter,
But a bit of better butter,
  That would make my batter better."
So she bought a bit of butter,
  Better than her bitter butter,
And she put it in her batter,
  And the batter was not bitter.
So t'was better Betty Botter
  Bought a bit of better butter.

JACK SPRAT

1639

Jack Sprat could eat no fat, His wife could eat no lean, And so be-tween them both, you see, They licked the plat-ter clean.

SEE-SAW, MARGERY DAW

1765

J. W. Elliott

See-saw, Mar-ger-y Daw, Jack shall have a new mas-ter, He shall have but a pen-ny a day, Be-cause he won't work an-y fast-er.

PAT-A-CAKE

1698

Pat-a-cake, pat-a-cake, ba—ker's man,

Bake me a cake just as fast as you can;

Pat it and prick it and mark it with B, Put

it in the o-ven for ba-by and me, For

ba-by and me, for ba-by and me, Put

it in the o-ven for ba-by and me.

33

THREE LITTLE KITTENS

1843

1. Once three lit-tle kit-tens they lost their mit-tens, And

they be-gan to cry, "Oh moth-er dear, we

sad-ly fear our mit-tens we have lost." "What!

lost your mit-tens? You naugh-ty kit-tens! Then

you shall have no pie." —— "Mee - ow,

Mee - ow, Mee - ow, Meow." ——

2. The three little kittens they found their mittens,
   And they began to cry,
   "Oh, mother dear, see here, see here,
   Our mittens we have found."
   "What! found your mittens, you darling kittens,
   Then you shall have some pie."
   "Mee-ow, mee-ow, mee-ow, meow."

3. The three little kittens put on their mittens,
   And soon ate up the pie;
   "Oh, mother dear, we greatly fear
   "Our mittens we have soiled."
   "What! soiled your mittens? You naughty kittens!"
   Then they began to sigh.
   "Mee-ow, mee-ow, mee-ow, meow."

4. The three little kittens they washed their mittens,
   And hung them up to dry;
   Oh, mother dear, look here, look here,
   Our mittens we have washed."
   "What! washed your mittens? You darling kittens,
   But I smell a rat close by."
   "Mee-ow, mee-ow, mee-ow, meow."

LITTLE TOMMY TUCKER

1744   J. W. Elliott

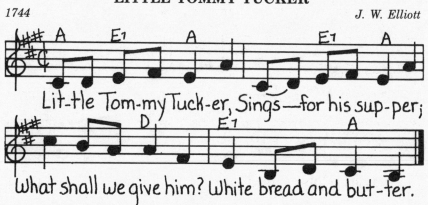

Lit-tle Tom-my Tuck-er, Sings—for his sup-per;

What shall we give him? White bread and but-ter.

LUCY LOCKET

1815

Lu-cy Lock-et lost her pock-et,

Kit-ty Fish-er found it; Not a pen-ny

was there in it, On-ly rib-bon 'round it.

LITTLE JACK HORNER

J. W. Elliott

1725

Lit-tle Jack Hor-ner sat in a cor-ner,

Eat-ing his Christ-mas pie;—He put in his thumb and

pulled out a plum, And said, "What a good boy am I!"—

LITTLE MISS MUFFET

1805

Lit-tle Miss Muf-fet sat on a tuf-fet,

Eat-ing her curds and whey;— A-

long came a spi-der who sat down be-side her, And

fright-ened Miss Muf-fet a-way.—

PETER PIPER

Peter Piper picked a peck of
  pickled peppers;
A peck of pickled peppers Peter
  Piper picked;
If Peter Piper picked a peck of
  pickled peppers,
Where's the peck of pickled peppers
  Peter Piper picked?

OH WHERE, OH WHERE HAS MY LITTLE DOG GONE?

S. W. 1864   *Septimus Winner*

Oh where, oh where has my lit-tle dog gone? Oh

where, oh where can he be? With his

ears cut short and his tail cut long, Oh

where, oh where can he be?

HIGGLETY, PIGGLETY

Higglety, pigglety, pop!
The dog has eaten the mop;
   The pig's in a hurry,
   The cat's in a flurry,
Higglety, pigglety, pop!

FIDDLE-DE-DEE

W. Crane 1879

1. Fid-dle-de-dee, Fid-dle-de-dee, The
fly has mar-ried the bum-ble-bee. Said the
fly, said he, "Will you mar-ry me? And
live with me, sweet bum-ble-bee?"
Fid-dle-de-dee, Fid-dle-de-dee, The
fly has mar-ried the bum-ble-bee.

2. Said the bee, said she, "I'll live under your wing,
   And you'll never know I carry a sting."
Fiddle-de-dee, fiddle-de-dee,
   The fly has married the bumblebee.
3. So when Parson Beetle had married the pair,
   They both went out to take the air...
4. And the flies did buzz, and the bells did ring—
   Did you ever hear so merry a thing?...

39

HEY DIDDLE DIDDLE

English 1765   *J. W. Elliott*

Hey did-dle did-dle, the cat and the fid-dle, The

cow jumped o - ver the moon; —— The

lit-tle dog laughed—to see such sport, And the

dish ran a- way with the spoon. ——

OLD KING COLE

1708   *1700s*

Old King Cole was a mer-ry old soul, and a

mer-ry old soul was he; He-called for his pipe, and he

40

called for his bowl, and he called for his fid-dlers-three.

Ev—'ry — fid-dler — had — a — fid-dle, And a

ver-y fine — fid-dle had he; Twee-dle

dee, twee-dle dee, went the fid-dlers-three, And so

mer-ry we — will — be.

HUMPTY DUMPTY

1700s

Hump-ty Dump-ty sat on a wall,

Hump-ty Dump-ty had a great fall;

All the king's hors-es and all the king's men

Could-n't put Hump-ty to-geth-er a-gain.

HICKETY, PICKETY, MY BLACK HEN

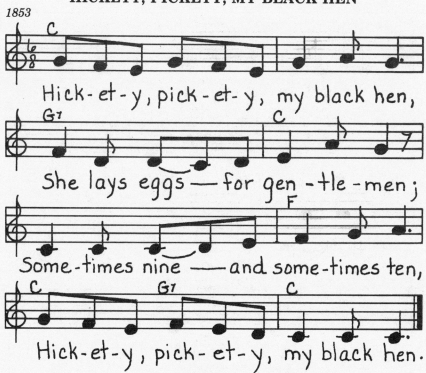

1853

Hick-et-y, pick-et-y, my black hen,

She lays eggs — for gen -tle-men;

Some-times nine — and some-times ten,

Hick-et-y, pick-et-y, my black hen.

HOT CROSS BUNS

Hot cross buns ! Hot cross buns !

One a pen-ny, two a pen-ny, Hot cross buns !

THERE WAS AN OLD WOMAN

English 1765
Irish 1600s

There was an old wo-man tossed up in a

bas-ket, Sev-en-teen times as high as the

moon; And where she was go-ing I could-n't but

ask it, For in her hand she car-ried a broom." Old

wo-man, old wo-man, old wo-man," said I, "Oh

whith-er, oh whith-er, oh whith-er so high?" "To

sweep—the cob—webs off—the sky."—"May

I— go with you?" "Aye, by and by."

TO BABYLAND

1800s   *English*

F

1. How man-y miles to Ba-by-land?

Bb   C7   F   Gm   C7

An-y-one can tell;— Up one flight,

F   Dm Gm   C7   F

To the right, Please to ring the bell.—

2. What do they do in Babyland?
   Dream and wake and play,
   Laugh and crow, fonder grow,
   Jolly times have they.

3. What do they say in Babyland?
   Why, the oddest things;
   Might as well try to tell
   What the birdie sings.

4. Who is the queen in Babyland?
   Mother, kind and sweet;
   And her love, born above,
   Guides the little feet.

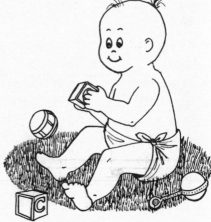

TWINKLE, TWINKLE, LITTLE STAR

Jane Taylor 1806   *English*

1. Twin-kle, twin-kle, lit-tle star, how I won-der what you are. Up a-bove the world so high, like a dia-mond in the sky, Twin-kle, twin-kle, lit-tle star, how I won-der what you are.

2. When the blazing sun is gone,
   When he nothing shines upon,
   Then you show your little light,
   Twinkle, twinkle all the night,
   Twinkle, twinkle, little star,
   How I wonder what you are.

3. Then the traveller in the dark,
   Thanks you for your tiny spark,
   He could not see where to go,
   If you did not twinkle so,
   Twinkle, twinkle, little star,
   How I wonder what you are.

4. In the dark blue sky you keep,
   Often through my curtains peep,
   For you never shut your eye,
   Till the sun is in the sky,
   Twinkle, twinkle, little star,
   How I wonder what you are.

Lullabies

ALL THROUGH THE NIGHT

Sir Harold Boulton 1884   *Welsh*

1. Sleep, my child, and peace at-tend thee,
All through the night; Guard-ian an-gels
God will send thee, All through the night;
Soft the drow-sy hours are creep-ing
Hill and vale in slum-ber steep-ing, I my lov-ing
vi-gil keep-ing, All through the night.

2. While the moon her watch is keeping,
   All through the night;
   While the weary world is sleeping,
   All through the night,
   O'er thy spirit gently stealing,
   Visions of delight revealing,
   Breathes a pure and holy feeling,
   All through the night.

WEE WILLIE WINKIE

Wee Willie Winkie
  Runs through the town,
Upstairs and downstairs,
  In his nightgown,
Rapping at the window,
  Crying through the lock,
"Are the children in their beds?
  Now it's eight o'clock."

ROCK-A-BYE, BABY

1765   *English*

Rock-a-bye, ba-by, on the tree top,
When the wind blows, the cra-dle will rock,
When the bough breaks, the cra-dle will fall, And
down will come ba-by, Cra-dle and all.

49

ARMENIAN LULLABY

Sleep, my lit-tle one, my — loved one,

As I rock and sing,

As the bright — moon wat-ches o'er us,

O'er your lit-tle crib.

BYE, BABY BUNTING

1784

Bye, — ba-by bunt-ing, Dad-dy's gone a-

hunt—ing, To get a lit-tle rab-bit skin, To

wrap his ba-by bunt-ing in.

MY DOLLY

Clara Belle Baker

German air

1. I've a dear lit-tle dol-ly; She has eyes of bright blue;
She can o-pen and shut them, and she smiles at me, too.

2. In the morning I dress her,
   And we go out to play,
   But I love best to rock her
   At the close of the day.

From *Songs for the Little Child.*
Copyright renewal 1949 by Clara Belle Baker.
Used by permission of the publisher, Abingdon Press.

ALL NIGHT, ALL DAY

1. All night, all — day, an-gels watch-in' o-ver
me, my Lord. — All night, all — day, an-gels
watch-in' o-ver me —

2. When at night I go to sleep,
   Angels watchin' over me, my Lord,
   Pray the Lord my soul to keep,
   Angels watchin' over me.

51

THE MOON

I see the moon
And the moon sees me;
God bless the moon,
And God bless me.

GOLDEN SLUMBERS

English 1600s

Gold—en slum-bers kiss your eyes,

Smiles — a - wake you when you rise,

Sleep, pret -ty loved—ones, do—not cry— And

I will sing a lul-la-by, Lul-la-by,

lul-la-by, lul————la-by.

HUSH, LITTLE BABY

English

1. Hush lit-tle ba-by, don't say a word,

Pa-pa's gon-na buy you a mock-ing bird.

2. If that mockingbird don't sing,
   Papa's gonna buy you a diamond ring.
3. If that diamond ring turns brass,
   Papa's gonna buy you a looking glass.
4. If that looking glass gets broke,
   Papa's gonna buy you a billy goat.
5. If that billy goat don't pull,
   Papa's gonna buy you a cart and bull.
6. If that cart and bull turn over,
   Papa's gonna buy you a dog named Rover.
7. If that dog named Rover don't bark,
   Papa's gonna buy you a horse and cart.
8. If that horse and cart fall down,
   You'll still be the sweetest little baby in town.

BYE, BYE, BABY

Pam Beall

Susan Nipp

Bye, bye, ba-by, hush-a-bye,

I will sing a lul-la-by.

Lul—la—by, do—not—cry,

Go to sleep my ba———by.

EARLY TO BED

Early to bed,
Early to rise,
Makes a man healthy,
Wealthy and wise.

MOZART'S LULLABY

W. A. Mozart

Sleep, lit-tle one, go to sleep, so peace-ful the birds and the sheep, Qui-et are mea-dow and trees, E-ven the buzz of the bees, The sil-ver-y moon-beams so bright, Down through the win-dow give light, O'er you the moon-beams will creep, Sleep lit-tle one go to sleep. Good night, ——— Good —— night.

LULLABY

Lul-la-by, lul-la-by, Do not wake and weep; Soft-ly in the cra-dle lie, sleep, O sleep. Soft-ly in the cra-dle lie, Sleep, my dar-ling, sleep

STAR LIGHT

Star light, star bright,
First star I see tonight,
I wish I may, I wish I might,
Have the wish I wish tonight.

56

GOOD NIGHT TO YOU ALL

Good-night to you all and sweet be your sleep; May an-gels a-round you their si-lent watch keep; Good night, good night, good-night, good-night.

HUSH MY CHILD

S.N.   *Susan Nipp*

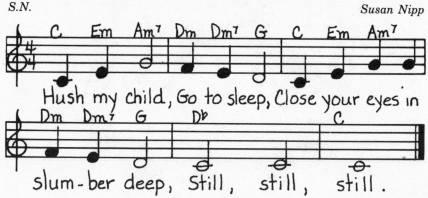

Hush my child, Go to sleep, Close your eyes in slum-ber deep, Still, still, still.

BRAHMS' LULLABY

Karl Simrock   *Johannes Brahms*

Lul-la-by and good-night, with—ros-es be-dight,— With— lil-ies be——spread is— ba——by's wee bed; Lay thee down now and rest, May thy slum-ber be blessed,— Lay thee down now and rest, May thy slum—ber be blessed.

HUSH-A-BYE

1. Hush a — bye, don't you — cry,
Lit - tle stars will see you.

2. Night is here, baby dear,
   You must go to sleep, too.

SLEEP, BABY, SLEEP

Sleep, ba - by, sleep. Your fa - ther tends the
sheep. Your moth - er shakes the dream - land tree, down
falls a lit - tle dream for thee. Sleep, ba - by, sleep.

ALL THE PRETTY LITTLE HORSES

American

Hush-a-bye, don't you cry, Go to sleep-y lit-tle
ba-by. Blacks and bays, dap-ples and grays,
coach and six-a-lit-tle hor-ses. Hush-a-bye,
don't you cry, Go to sleep-y lit-tle ba-by.

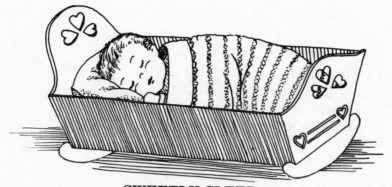

SWEETLY SLEEP

Ti-ny ba-by, sweet-ly—sleep, do not— weep,

Sleep in— com-fort,— slum-ber— deep.

I will rock you, rock you, rock you,

I will rock you, rock you, rock you,

Ti-ny ba-by sweet-ly — sleep,

Sleep in — com-fort — slum-ber —deep.

INDEX

Wee Sing®

by Pamela Conn Beall and Susan Hagen Nipp

Discover all the books and cassettes
in the best-selling WEE SING series!

WEE SING
WEE SING AND PLAY
WEE SING SILLY SONGS
WEE SING FOR CHRISTMAS
WEE SING NURSERY RHYMES AND LULLABIES
WEE SING BIBLE SONGS
WEE SING AMERICA
WEE SING SING-ALONGS
(formerly titled *Wee Sing Around the Campfire*)
WEE SING FUN 'N' FOLK
WEE SING OVER IN THE MEADOW
WEE SING DINOSAURS
WEE COLOR WEE SING AND PLAY
WEE COLOR WEE SING
WEE COLOR WEE SING SILLY SONGS
WEE COLOR WEE SING AROUND THE CAMPFIRE
WEE COLOR WEE SING BIBLE SONGS
WEE COLOR WEE SING AMERICA
WEE COLOR WEE SING AUSTRALIA
WEE COLOR WEE SING DINOSAURS
WEE COLOR WEE SING KING COLE'S PARTY
WEE COLOR WEE SING TOGETHER
WEE COLOR WEE SING FOR CHRISTMAS

And now, experience the excitement of our magical musical videos

WEE SING TOGETHER
KING COLE'S PARTY
GRANDPA'S MAGICAL TOYS
WEE SING IN SILLYVILLE
WEE SING THE BEST CHRISTMAS EVER
WEE SING IN THE BIG ROCK CANDY MOUNTAINS

The above titles are available wherever books are sold or
can be ordered directly from the publisher.

PRICE STERN SLOAN

11150 Olympic Boulevard, Suite 650, Los Angeles, California 90064
Printed and assembled in M